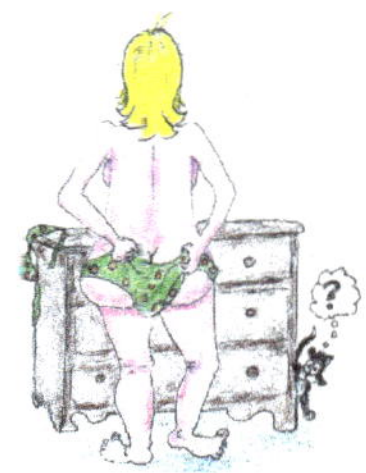

Illustrated American Idioms

Book 2

A Bad Actor

a phrase that is used when describing an unruly, unreliable person (who has a hidden agenda of disruption) and who causes trouble wherever he or she goes

Example: "There are a few of the kids in your new class who are ***bad actors***. I hope you are ready to deal with the problems they'll be creating!"

A Bad Influence

someone who encourages wrong actions and/or thoughts by their poor examples (also known as "a bad apple"...."a bad egg"...." a bad actor")

Example: "Pete, the pot smoker, is a bad example to the younger kids at our school. He is leading them down a rocky road, by his poor example and illegal choices. He's ***a bad influence*** for all of the youngsters!

A Big Cheese

someone who has power and control over others....(also known as "a big wig" and "a top dog")

Example: "Charlie had control over the West Side of our city. If you wanted something, you had to go through Charlie. He was ***the big cheese***!"

A Big Fish In A Small Pond

a term used to describe when a person who has demonstrated superior qualities in an environment where there are fewer people to compete with….in another larger community, there will be much more competition (and many bigger fish)

Example: "Heather thinks she's so good at translating Latin. Wait until she gets to college, and the new group she studies with all have better developed skills in that area. Right now she is ***a big fish in a small pond***!"

A Bird In Hand Is Worth Two In The Bush

it's better to hold onto something that you have, than to risk losing it, when reaching for something that you see as better

Example: "Jake lost the twenty dollar bill that he found at the river's edge, when he reached for two more in the water. He fell into the river instead! That just goes to show you that ***a bird in hand is worth two in the bush***!"

A Blue Hair

this idiom is used to describe any elderly woman who has tinted her hair with a solution (white mink tint) so as to cover up any grey/yellow hairs

Example: "I saw two ***blue hairs*** running to the St. Paul's Bingo parlor last night. They almost ran me over! What's the matter with old ladies these days?"

A Bozo

used to describe someone who is foolish and incompetent

Example: "Phil's wife bought him a new coat and pants set that looked like striped pajamas. He hated the look. It made him feel like a ***real bozo***!"

A Bundle Of Nerves

a term used to describe a person who is extremely nervous and fit to be tied because of their behavior

Example: "They had to take the clerk at CVS to the hospital this afternoon. An angry customer was so upset, that he had mistakenly sold her nerve medication to some other customer, that she over reacted. She was ***a bundle of nerves*** and very irate!"

A Bushel And a Peck

this idiom is used to describe whenever someone loves someone very much

Example: “Great grandfather loves little Rosalie so much. They both love each other ***a bushel and a peck.***”

G. JACKMAN

A Piece Of Cake

........a task or job that is viewed as very easy

Example: "Constantine thought the German Language class would be a ***piece of cake***."

A Sweet Tooth

this American idiom is used to describe whenever someone loves sugar and can never have enough

Example: "Arthur has a ***sweet tooth***. Whenever he eats sweets, his behaviors change. He can be a real problem for teachers. He is a different person altogether!"

Above The Law

this idiom is used to describe a person who feels that they are not required to follow the rules of society

Example: "I saw Tommy Twoface throwing bagged dog poo on the lawn again. He thinks he is ***above the law***, just because his father is the Chief Of Police in our town."

Ace In The Hole

an advantage that you have that other people do not know about

Example: "Our basketball squad has an ***ace in the hole*** with our new center. Other teams will be quite surprised at his size, speed, and ability!"

All Ears

to be very interested in hearing all the details about something

Example: "Alfred was ***all ears***, when Charlie started talking about what happened, when the police came to the neighborhood last night!"

As Easy As A B C

to be very easy…(also known as “a piece of cake”, “a breeze”, “a walk in the park”, and “a cake walk”)

Example: “Rob’s new teachers soon found out that their jobs were no longer ***as easy as ABC***!

As The Bird Flies

……..also "as the crow flies"…used to describe the shortest route from one place to another

Example: "It's 40 minutes by bus from here to Boston. ***As the bird flies***, it's only 20 minutes."

Bad News Travels Fast

people spread news about bad events very quickly

Example: "Did you hear about Dave Mcgee driving drunk, and broadsiding a State Police Cruiser? He won't be driving around for a long time. **Bad news travels fast**."

Bag And Baggage

an American idiom that is used to describe whenever someone shows up somewhere with everything that they own.

Example: Anita arrived today, unannounced. She was on my door step ***bag and baggage***."

Ball And Chain

a heavy attachment that weighs one down

Example: "Walter can't seem to meet his quota lately. I think his new assignment is ***a ball and chain***! It seems like he has no energy anymore."

Barking Up The Wrong Tree

to be persistently focused on a wrong solution to solve a problem

Example: "Bill is putting all his effort into impressing Caroline with his basketball playing. She would take more notice if he concentrated on his academic standing. If you ask me, I think he is ***barking up the wrong tree***!."

Be In One's Element

to be very comfortable doing something that comes naturally to you

Example: "Maxine is ***in her element*** when she is playing tennis! She makes playing the game look easy!"

Beat Around The Bush

this American Idiom is used to describe whenever someone is not speaking directly, but instead, talking in a roundabout cautious manner

Example: "Anthony, will you stop ***beating around the bush*** and get to the point!"

Bending The Rules

whenever someone is not following the spirit of a law, but instead, being sneaky and appearing to follow the intent of a law

Example: "Tommy the dog walker does a great job picking up the mess and placing it in a plastic bag. Then, instead of throwing the bagged poop into a disposal container he throws it back onto the ground! Now that is ***bending the rules*** for sure!"

Bent Out Of Shape

to become very angry or upset (also known as "to blow one's stack")

Example: "Norm was so ***bent out of shape***, with the bill that he received from his therapist, that he blew his stack!"

Between The Devil And The Deep Blue Sea

any dilemma that puts a person in the hard place of choosing between a bad situation or one that is just as bad or worse….also known as "between a rock and a hard place"

Example: "Jacob has to choose between baseball and soccer at school, in order to graduate. He hates both of those sports! He is stuck with a choice between ***the devil and the deep blue sea***."

Big Wig

a very important person....the most important person in a group or undertaking...(also known as "top banana", "big cheese", "top gun", and "heavy hitter")

Example: "Zelda is the person you should talk to about this account. She is the ***big wig*** for that company!."

Bigger Fish To Fry

this idiom is used to describe whenever anyone has something more important to get done

Example: "Daniel had to stop his search for the masked paper boy, who was knocking mail boxes over with a baseball bat. The call came in that there was an armed robbery at the downtown bank. He now had ***bigger fish to fry***!"

Birds OF A Feather Flock Together

similar people have similar likes and dislikes, go to the same places and do the same things together

Example: "Larry enjoys betting on the horses. Bill, Sam, Harry and Howie do too! They sure are ***birds of a feather***. It's no wonder they are always seen with each other!"

Birthday Suit

a term used to describe when a person is totally naked (like the day they were born)

Example: "Mary Anne got the bottom of her bikini on, just as her boyfriend came into the room! If he had entered 30 seconds earlier, he would have seen her in her ***birthday suit***!"

Bite The Dust

to die

Example: "Pecos Pete ***bit the dust*** in a gunfight he lost yesterday, to a Texas Ranger from El Paso."

Bite Your Tongue

to struggle not to say something that you want to say because if you say it you will create some type of problem

Example: "Miss Jones had to ***bite her tongue*** when she saw that her boyfriend was using the wrong wrench to fix the sink."

Bits And Pieces

this idiom is used to describe an assortment of miscellaneous items (not used or useful anymore) also known as “odds and ends”

Example: “Judy and Tammy were trying to decide what to do with their ***bits and pieces*** before their big move to Florida.”

Black Sheep

this American idiom describes whenever a family member is disreputable within his (or her) family

Example: "Mortimer was considered the ***black sheep*** of his family because he drank too much, ran around with the wrong crowd, and joined the army instead of attending college (like the rest of the family)!

Blend Into The Woodwork

to fit in so well that one can easily go unnoticed....to be chameleon-like

Example: "Freddie is such a social person. Wherever he goes, he seems to ***blend into the woodwork!"***

To Be Blind Sided

this American Idiom is used to describe whenever someone is startled or surprised and could not see something or someone who was about to hurt them

Example: "Miss Bradshaw was ***blind sided*** by a mugger who ran off with her purse and all her credit cards!"

A Blockhead

this idiom is used to describe a person who acts stupid or foolish

Example: "Bill is ***a blockhead***! He keeps loaning Charlie money (that Charlie never gives back!) When is he going to learn?"

Blood, Sweat, And Tears

this idiom is used to describe whenever there is an action or project that will take a lot of human effort and sacrifice

Example: "Sam was a hard-working farmer. Whatever he did, he did it well. When people would ask him how his crops were always the best, he would tell them, 'With the help of the Good Lord , and a lot of my ***blood, sweat, and tears***!'"

Blow A Fuse

to explode with anger

Example: "Our basketball coach ***blew a fuse*** in the locker room at half time, because of the way our team played!"

Boob Tube

an American alternative name for the television

...the name implies that continuous watching of T.V. will make you stupid and misinformed

Example: "The only information these kids get is from the ***boob tube***!"

Born With A Silver Spoon In His Mouth

this American idiom is used to describe whenever someone comes from a wealthy family

Example: "Arthur doesn't know the meaning of hard work! He was ***born with a silver spoon in his mouth***. Everything is given to him."

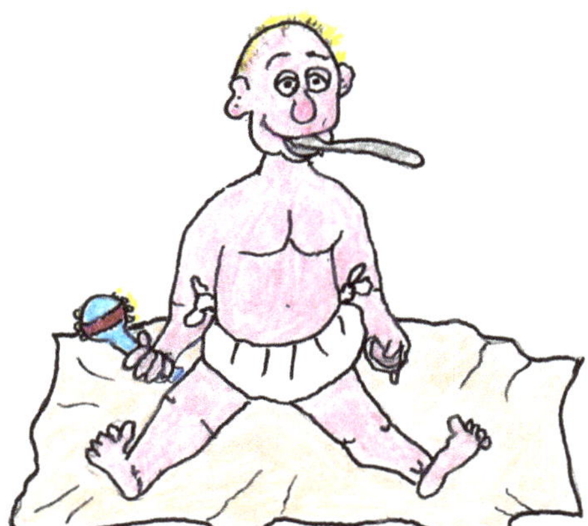

Card Shark

this idiom refers to an expert card player.... a professional (who might have a card or two up his sleeve, giving him an unfair advantage)

Example: "Texas Pete in a genuine *card shark*. He's a gambler, who wins all the games with his expertise. He plays his cards close to the vest, and, he can bluff like no other card player!"

Catch Someone's Eye

to be attractive to someone else

Example: "Mimi the pup ***caught Fido's eye*** this morning!"

Caught Between A rock And Hard Place

this idiom is used to describe whenever a person is faced with choosing between two equally unpleasant courses of action

Example: "Larry is either going to serve time in juvenile lock-up, or, be placed in a psychiatric observation and treatment facility, for all the trouble he has caused in school this semester! He's ***caught between a rock and a hard place***."

Chew The Fat

to talk about anything just to pass the time.....to waste time on "small talk" that isn't really important

Example: "The kids at my college would sit around the campfire, and drink beer, and trade jokes, and ***chew the fat***, until the fire went out."

Chicken Feed

a very small amount of money....also known as "small potatoes" and "peanuts"

Example: "Hans was saving to buy a car, but it was difficult, because he was working for ***chicken feed***."

Circle The Wagons

to form a circle of protection against "outside" dangers.....to pull together in a common cause to defend against perceived dangers

Example: "When Paul's dad lost his job, the family had to ***circle the wagons*** and tight their budget!"

Clouds On The Horizon

this idiom means trouble is coming

Example: "Standing on the shoreline, one member of the native tribe spotted a very big canoe that he had never seen before. He also saw ***clouds on the horizon***! He knew that trouble was on the way."

Cold Shoulder

to ignore someone.....to act unfriendly

Example: "Sally the fashionista was giving every one that she walked by the ***cold shoulder***. Who does she think she is, the Queen Of Fashion?

Cold Turkey

to quit something abruptly, on the spot

Example: "Jake smoked cigarettes for 33 years. Then, one day he just kicked the habit. He stopped ***cold turkey***!"

Couch Potato

a very lazy or idle person who sits around all day watching the television

Example: "Calvin is out in the front room watching the television. That's all he ever does. He's a real ***couch potato***!"

Cover All The Bases

an idiom that is used to describe whenever someone attempts to prepare for every possibility

Example: "We don't want to have to go to court about this! We need to ***cover all the bases*** to make sure that we haven't overlooked something.

Create A Stink

to make a major issue out of something small....to make a lot of complaints and criticisms about something that you don't agree with

Example: "Our ward representative is ***creating a stink*** over the new hotel that they want to build on the river's edge!"

Crocodile Tears

to pretend to weep or cry (to show an insincere sadness) in order to manipulate another person

Example: "Judy is always getting her own way. She knows that all she has to do is cry ***crocodile tears,*** and everything will go according to her hidden agenda."

Cross Your Fingers

a superstition that people use (in hopes that things will turn out the way they want them to)

Example: "One more game and out team will win the title. ***Cross your fingers***!"

Crunch Time

a crucial decision has to be made, immediately

Example: "Jake had to get the ball to Josh, so that he could shoot the three-pointer, to win the game.
With one second left on the clock, it was ***crunch time***!"

Culture Shock

feeling uncomfortable in a strange country or place because of the unfamiliar habits and ways of life

Example: "I think William is feeling some ***culture shock*** since his enrollment in the new inner-city school."

Cut That Out

an American idiom that means “Stop!” (also known as “Knock It Off!” and “Cut The Crap!”)

Example: “Hey Joe! Those boxes aren’t going to move themselves. Stop fooling around on the job. ***Cut that out***!”

Cut-Throat

this idiom is used to describe whenever a person wants success so badly, that they do not care who they harm to get it

Example: "Sandy is a self-centered ***cut throat***. He will stop at nothing to succeed. He does not care who he hurts, just as long as long as he has his way!"

Cutting Up

this idiom is used to describe when a student is misbehaving, being naughty, or out of control in order to get attention (or to steal the focus of others)

Example: "Junior was ***cutting up*** in school again today! Miss Cranky caught him flying his airplane and marking up his desk! She sent him to the Principal's Office for detention!"

Day Dreaming

this idiom describes whenever a person is thinking about things that he (or she) would love to be doing (or wished they had done) instead of focusing on what is happening in the real world

Example: “Papa missed his opportunity to get free Red Sox tickets yesterday. Instead, he was ***day dreaming*** about the family, and how much he was missing them.”

Dead As A Doornail

this idiom refers to something that cannot be re-used....doornails used to be hammered into the wood from the outside of a door, then they were bent over from the inside to be more secure (this was called "clenching") once clenching occurred, the doornails were "dead" and could never be used again...in our present time the idiom is used to describe anything that stops working

Example: "Robert's car battery is as ***dead as a doornail***. He can't get the car to start. He will have to buy a new battery."

Dead Presidents

(also known as “greenbacks”) this term is used to describe American paper money

Example: “Bill paid cash for his motor cycle; eight hundred and fifty five dollars in ***dead presidents***!”

Dig In

this idiom means that somebody can (and should) begin to eat a meal

Example: "When we were growing up we had to sit around the supper table and wait for our father to sit down. He would smile at his five children; he would thank our mother for preparing the meal; he would give thanks for our blessings; and then proclaim ***'Dig In!'*** "

Dog Eat Dog

a phrase meaning that people will do anything to be successful (even if it means hurting other people)

Example: "This morning the boss fired four of the salesmen, because they couldn't meet their numbers. Just last week he took over their territory for his own. It's a ***dog eat dog*** world out there!"

Don't Judge A Book By Its' Cover

an idiom used to describe whenever anyone passes their value judgement on another person because of the way they dress and/or comb their hair

Example: "George didn't care that the kid dressed like a Neo-Nazi. He knew him from childhood and that he was a brave, courageous, and bold individual. ***'Don't judge a book by its' cover!'*** George would say!"

Don't Rain On My Parade

a phrase that asks someone not to spoil your fun with some bad news (also known as "to put a damper on" on your happiness)

Example: "We were having a great time, until Alex came over, and gave us the latest news, about the evictions being served in the neighborhood. I wish he ***didn't rain on my parade***! It ruined my day."

Down In The Dumps

this idiom is used to show when someone becomes overly depressed and lonely

Example: "Skipper was lost, scared, and lonely. He was really ***down in the dumps***!

Draw A Blank

the inability to remember or recall something (also known as "brain freeze")

Example: "Zeke studied all night for the Latin test. But when the time came, he just ***drew a blank***!"

Draw The Short Straw

to have to do an undesirable task because of all the straws offered, yours was the shortest

Example: "It looks like George has to mow the lawn this time. He ***drew the short straw***!"

Drop The Ball

an American idiom that is used to describe whenever someone blunders their part in an organization

Example: "Freddie left last night, without getting the needed signatures on the contract. In his haste and carelessness, he ***dropped the ball*** on that sweet deal."

Drown Your Sorrows

this idiom refers to someone who is very sad and lonely and chooses to use alcohol to escape their pain

Example: "Barney can be found down at Willie's Bar ***drowning his sorrows***. He will sit there, drinking gin, until closing time.

Drum Up Support

this idiom is used to describe whenever anyone goes out to talk to people or groups of people to arouse and enlist their support for a cause or action

Example: "Ralph went door to door presenting his arguments to our town's tax payers so that he could ***drum up support*** for votes in the coming elections."

Eat My Hat

people use this expression when they don't believe that something is going to happen

Example: "Last Thursday Diane told Steve that she and he were signed up to take ballroom dance lessons on Friday night. 'I'll ***eat my hat*** before I go to those lessons!' Steve replied. By 10 o'clock Friday night, Diane and Steve were wrapping up their first ballroom dancing lesson! Steve needs to get a new hat!"

Elbow Room

to have enough room or space to feel comfortable and uncrowded

Example: "The County has added 100 more feet to the meeting room. That way people will feel they have a little more ***elbow room***!"

Empty Vessels Make The Most Noise

thoughtless people often speak the most

Example: "When John comes to the party he is the loudest talker. He doesn't think much, but that doesn't stop him. Half the stuff he says is untrue or imaginary. His pal Bud is the same way! ***Empty vessels make the most noise*** !"

Even A Blind Squirrel Finds A Nut Once In A While

even if people are ineffective or misguided, sometimes they can be lucky and succeed

Example: "Raul couldn't hold a note in a bucket! The only song that he sounded good singing was the Star Spangled Banner. The Principal of our school heard him one day and asked if would sing at our graduation. ***Even a blind squirrel finds a nut once in a while***."

Every Ass Loves To Hear Himself Bray

people like the sound of their own voice

Example: "Gerald sounds like a donkey. Nobody wants to be in his company! No one can get a word in edge-wise. ***Every ass loves to hear himself bray*** ."

Eyeball To Eyeball

...... face to face, nose to nose with somebody, especially in an aggressive and direct way

Example: "Mike and Bud were arguing ***eyeball to eyeball*** over who forgot to check the gas when they ran out on the way to a concert."

Fat Cat

this idiom is used to show when someone is rich, powerful, self-satisfied, and who lives in excess (also known as living ***High Off The Hog***)

Example: “Those big oil company C.E.O.s aren’t worried about the high cost of gas and oil. They are just ***fat cats*** who love their lifestyle of living ***high off the hog***!”

Fill Someone's Shoes

to replace someone else.....to do the job that they used to do so well

Example: "Jenny left for California yesterday. It will be hard to replace her. It will be tough to ***Fill Her Shoes***!"

Firecracker

a term used to describe a very energetic person who is extremely active in whatever they do

Example: "Sally can dance the jitterbug for ten hours straight. She's a real ***firecracker***!"

Fit As A Fiddle

to be in good shape....healthy and ready to go

Example: "Old Joe Clark is as fit as a fiddle! How does he stay in such good health?"

Follow Your Heart

this idiom refers to someone who follows their bliss.....to do what their feelings tell them to do.....to obey their inner compassionate self

Example: "Rita is always so happy when her students succeed. You can tell that she is a very good teacher. She always gives a lot of thought to her lesson plans. That's because ***she follows her heart*** and meets all of her unique students learning styles."

For The Birds

this idiom is used to describe when something is without real value (birds eat seed, and seed is not a lot to eat)

Example: "I agree with you, Calvin. This new school system plan is ***for the birds***! It shows no real value for the money that it is going to cost!"

Frequent Flyer

this idiom is used to describe whenever a person's poor behavioral choices repeatedly get him (or her) into trouble with authority figures

Example: "Nimrod is always in detention at our high school. His skipping classes, never doing his homework, smoking in the boiler room, and playing pranks on teachers are his modus operandi. The principal calls him a ***frequent flyer*** !

A Front Runner

a person or thing most likely to win or succeed

Example: "Felicia's famous Boston Cream Pie is the *front runner* in this year's judging at the Food Fair, in the sweets division!!"

Full Of Bologna

Whenever someone exaggerates...stretches the truth...embellishes a story

Example: "Pat is so ***full of bologna***. He stretches that story more, every time he tells it! He is always telling ***tall tales***!"

Game Plan

to come up with a strategy for succeeding in a business venture or a sporting event

Example: "Zeke and Joshua were given the responsibility to come up with a ***game plan*** for the following day's meeting."

Get A Kick Out Of Something

to find something humorous....(also known as "to tickle your funny bone")

Example: "Gaston ***gets a kick out of*** the antics of his new kitten, Ned!"

Get Cold Feet

when somebody suddenly becomes too frightened to do something that they had planned to do

Example: "Steve was getting married on Sunday. At the last minute he ***got cold feet***."

To Get In Line

to form a line or a row……..to conform, adhere to…….to agree with rules and behaviors

Example: "If those geese don't ***get into line*** now, they will never make it to the South until after Winter!"

To Get The Run Around

to receive a series of excuses, delays, and/or referrals

Example: "I'm sick and tired of calling that company to ask about my refund. They ***keep giving me the run around***!"

To Get Your Act Together

this idiom refers to a person who is warned to quit playing around ….. to start doing what is expected

Example: "Maxx, our stage director, is always telling us to stop goofing around; ***to get our act together***!"

Give A Fig

this idiom is used to show if someone is interested in something.....if someone cares about something

Example: "Barney doesn't care about that mail box issue! He's not interested in the petty stuff. He doesn't *give a fig* about it!"

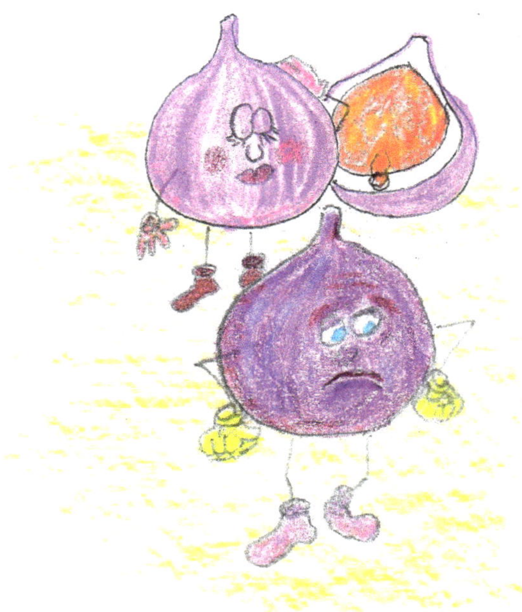

Give The Evil Eye

to look at someone in an unpleasant way usually followed by doing harm to that someone

Example: "The worm that I use on my fishing hook must have the power to *give the evil eye* to the fish. I haven't had a bite all morning!"

Go Down In Flames

this idiom is used to describe whenever something (or someone) fails spectacularly

Example: "The last I saw of Eddy was when he was ***going down in flames***. I don't know if he made it safely to the ground or not

Gobbledegook

complicated, meaningless, obscure language

Example: "That stuff that Constantine is reading in biology class is pure ***gobbledegook***! He would be better to learn some good old fashioned American Idioms."

Gone Pear Shaped

this American idiom describes when something goes badly wrong

Example: "Everything was fine until Alice showed up on the job. Then it all started to go wrong. By the second day, everything had *gone pear shaped*!"

Good Things Come To Those Who Wait

this idiom is used to encourage people to show patience

Example: "Bill wanted to buy that car over at Benny's Car Sales, but Benny was asking too much. Bill kept working and saving, hoping that the price would drop. Last Friday, when Bill passed Benny's Car Sales, he saw that the price was one thousand dollars cheaper! Bill went in and purchased the car with cash. ***Good things come to those who wait***!"

Half-Assed

to do a task or job that falls very short of all expectations....not doing the best that one can do

Example: "It is a wonder that Joe the plumber has stayed in business all these years! Everything he fixes is done in a ***half-assed*** manner!"

Handy Man

a person who has the skills to be able to fix just about anything that could go wrong around the house

Example: "My nephew, Bill, is a carpenter, plumber, mason, and an electrician! When it comes to house repairs, he is a real ***handy man***."

Happy As A Clam

comfortable with life just the way it is

Example: "Jose and Anna Maria are as ***happy as clams*** in their new marriage!"

Head Over Heels (In Love)

seeing someone who knocks you off your feet....falling in love at first sight

Example: "Christine fell ***head over heels*** for Billy when she first saw him!"

Head To Head

any dilemma that describes a person in a close contact combat situation….also known as "Nose To Nose"

Example: "My father and I used to go ***head to head***, every Saturday night, over my walking to the dance or my using the family car!" The only times I would come out on top was when he would let me."

Hit The Hay

to go to bed at any time of the day or night (also known as "Hit The Sack" and "Catch A Few Zs")

Example: "Luke ***hit the hay*** early tonight. He had three tough days, working 12 hours each day. He must be very tired."

Hit The Nail On The Head

to do exactly the right thing.....to do something in the most effective and most efficient way

Example: "Will's Candy Apple Red paint job really gave his car the appearance of a hot rod! He ***hit the nail on the head*** with his choice of color!"

Hitting The Books

to work very hard in your studies....to study hard for an examination

Example: "Hermann is up in the study ***hitting the books*** for his final exam."

Home Sweet Home

this idiom is used to describe whenever a person comes home to a place of rest, relaxation, and good food.....sanctuary from the rest of the world

Example: "Tony came home, after a hard day's work, to find that his wife had made his favorite cookies. He rested his weary head on her shoulders and sighed, *'Home Sweet Home'*. His wife smiled; happy that he showed his appreciation."

The Honcho

an American idiom that describes who is in charge (also known as “boss”’…”top banana”)

Example: “Charlie was puzzled. Why was he the man up on the ladder? Why wasn’t it Bob? After all, Charlie was ***the honcho***.”

Hot-Dogging

this idiom is used to describe whenever a person performs daring, showy, flamboyant and intricate stunts to impress others

Example: "Danny was out there on his skate board ***hot-dogging*** in front of all the girls today. He is so into himself!"

Humble Pie

to be upset that something you said or did was proven to be wrong (causing you shame and embarrassment, hurting your pride)

Example: "Zack was really embarrassed, when his boss found out about his failure to meet his quota (after he had promised that he could do it!) Zack had to eat some ***humble pie***. He wasn't happy."

In The Driver's Seat

when one is in complete control.....when one has total charge of things

Example: "Now that Jacob is ***in the driver's seat***, people can't wait to see how quickly the company will change ."

In The Same Boat

people who are in a similar situation or circumstance

Example: "Bill, Jack, Dave, and Albert are all ***in the same boat***. They were caught smoking in the boiler room at school and were suspended for a week!"

In This Neck Of The Woods

an idiom that means "in some particular vicinity or neighborhood" (usually in a place where one would not be seen)

Example: "Mr. Brown never comes to Newburyport's South End! I wonder why he is ***in this neck of the woods***?"

It Cost An Arm And A Leg

this idiom is used to describe the purchase of something very expensive....much more expensive than expected

Example: "Dad couldn't get over how much money it cost for a peck of apples and a dozen fresh sugar-coated doughnuts! When he got to the cider drinks, he started complaining about the trip ***costing him an arm and a leg***!"

It's In The Bag

to be guaranteed to win a contest…achievement assured

Example: "The Rabbi and his wife will win the first place dancing award, again this year. They are so good at the tango**.** ***It's in the bag***!

Jack Of All Trades

an American idiom that describes someone who seems to know many different trades

Example: "Charlie can fix anything! He can do carpentry, plumbing, auto mechanics, machine repair, heating and air conditioning. He is a multitalented individual. He's a ***jack of all trades***!"

Kick The Bucket

to die (also known as “To Pass On”, “To Cross Over”, “To Bite The Dust”, “To Go To The Last Round-up”)

Example: “Old Man Evens didn’t get to finish his boat. Before he had the last coat of paint on the hull, he ***kicked the bucket***.”

Kill Two Birds With One Stone

to achieve two aims through one action…solving two problems at the same time

Example: "Dad created three illustrated limericks while he sat in the doctor's office, waiting for Mom. He ***killed two birds with one stone***!"

Knee Jerk Reaction

to respond to something without giving it much thought.....a reflex motion

Example: "The Mayor's ***knee jerk reaction*** to the State's deadline demand cost the city $140,000 tax-payer dollars."

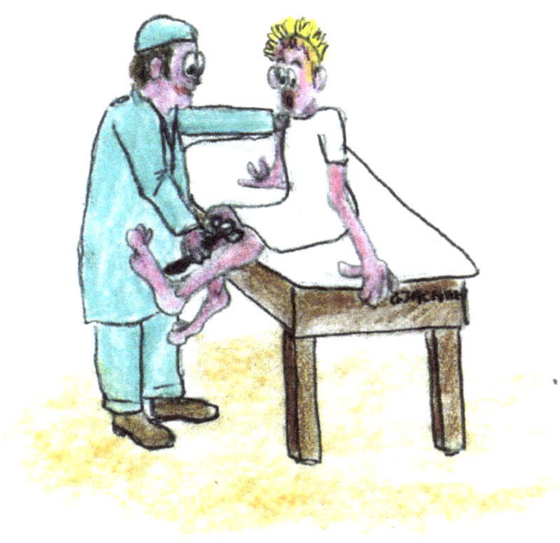

Lay Down The Law

a phrase used to explain whenever someone with authority uses their position to enforce the rules

Example: "Mr. Tootuff was out in the hallways this morning, making sure every student was following school rules. He thought it was a good time to
lay down the law to any miscreant who was misbehaving!"

Lazy Bones

this idiom describes when someone is not very productive and just seems to do nothing but sleep…..to have no drive

Example: "Barry's dog does nothing all day but lay around the house. Even when he is outside, he just looks for a place in the shade for a safe spot to rest. I guess that's why they called him ***Lazy Bones***."

Like Riding A Bike

when something is learned so well it seems easy to do

Example: "George went through that extremely difficult Spartan obstacle course ***like he was riding a bike***!"

Loan Shark

this idiom refers to an unscrupulous money lender, who loans money at a very unlawfully high rate of interest

Example: "Slick Fitzgerald is one of the worst money-lenders in the city. He'll charge you an arm and a leg for a loan. You would be wise to stay away from the likes of him. He's a *loan shark*. Find someone else to front you a loan for your candlestick holder business!"

Long Shot

this term is used to describe when something is not likely to succeed, but is worth a try

Example: "The chances of Freddie throwing a role of tape over his shoulder and getting it into the box are pretty slim. Most folks would call it a ***long shot***!"

Long In The Tooth

a phrase used to explain whenever someone is really old and has been around for a long time

Example: "Harold is older than dirt! He has been around the world and back again fifty times. He's like an old lion; ***long in the tooth***!

To Make The Rounds

- ....to go on a daily established routine of visits to certain places...to see friends....to shop....to get a bite to eat
- **Example:** "Aunt Betty may be old, but she ***still makes the rounds*** She walks five miles a day to visit her old classmates at the nursing home; She brings them candy and cigarettes; They talk about the good old days; Then she goes home feeling good!"

Make Up Your Mind

a term used to describe whenever anyone has to come to a decision about anything

Example: "It's hard for Alan to decide who he will take to the movies tonight. He is having a tough time ***making up his mind***!"

Making A Beeline

this idiom is used to describe whenever someone goes very quickly from one place to another, using the fastest route possible

Example: "I saw your aunt Millie and her friend, Betty, ***making a beeline*** for the bingo parlor yesterday. They looked like they were in a hurry!"

Mental Case

to be mentally unstable .... (also known as "a fruit cake", "a nut case", or "insane")

Example: "Mr. Johnson went crazy in the hallways this morning. He started shooting students with a stun gun, because they were listening to rap music on their head sets. He acted like a ***Mental Case***!"

Mind Your Own Business

a phrase used to tell someone (who is into everybody else's private business) that they are interfering in something that is not their concern ....that they are a busy body

Example: "Hunter never ***minds his own business***! He is a nosey busy body!"

Monkey See, Monkey Do

this idiom is used to describe whenever people tend to copy each other

Example: "Every time Rosie gets a new hat, Mary has to purchase one exactly like it! ***Monkey see, monkey do***!"

No Pain, No Gain

when you have a goal to meet, and, if you don't work very hard, you will not achieve it

Example: "Sally wants to lose 40 pounds before her daughter's wedding. That means she must keep away from sweets. ***No pain, no gain***!"

No Spring Chicken

a phrase used to explain when someone has grown older

Example: "Nellie looks so much older, since I've seen her last. She's still a beautiful woman, but she's ***no spring chicken*** any longer!"

Nosey

someone who is into everybody else's private business.....(also known as a "busy body")

Example: "Artie is always looking around for shocking news about others. He has no respect for people's privacy! He is just a busy body digging up dirt; he's ***nosey***!"

Nuts

to act crazy or whacky or foolishly….also known as "gone bananas" or "gone mad"

Example: "You shouldn't hang around with that group of ***nuts***. Everyone in town thinks that their choices of behaviors are crazy, and that sooner or later, they will be doing time in reform school!"

Nuts And Bolts

the most important practical aspect of something.....the most essential components of a piece (also known as "The Heart Of The Matter" or "The Real Nitty Gritty")

Example: "The ***nuts and bolts*** of her argument were in the very first paragraph of her presentation."

On Cloud Nine

this American idiom is used to describe whenever someone is blissfully happy…cheerful…delighted

Example: "Something very good must have happened to Harry. He's *on cloud nine* today!"

On The Ball

this idiom describes whenever someone is doing things the right way.....sharp.....on target.... efficient

Example: "Luca is so good at his work! I would say he is ***on the ball*** each and every day!"

One Bad Apple Can Cause The Rest To Spoil

this idiom describes when someone is a bad influence on others........one bad apple can really cause other apples in the basket to be overripe and to spoil

Example: "Jeff found a huge worm in the apple he had bitten into, yesterday, at the apple orchard. His friends all spit their apples out, and examined them closely! One of them said '***One bad apple can cause the rest to spoil!***'"

One Man's Trash Is Another Man's Treasure

what one person may consider worthless, another person could see as a highly prized item

Example: "Brett found a gas-powered lawn mower in the trash yesterday morning. By noon he had that machine up and running like a new mower. All it needed was a spark plug! Now that's why Brett is always saying ***One Man's Trash Is Another Man's Treasure***!"

One Smart Cookie

this idiom refers to someone who has shown themselves to be an exceptional learner with high intelligence

Example: "Felicia's youngest daughter is so talented. Besides being a hard-working student, she is a very good artist, singer, dancer, and a true athlete. She is ***one smart cookie***!"

One Tough Cookie

a term used to describe a strong, determined tough guy....not easily scared, discouraged or intimidated

Example: "I saw Joe, 'The Junkyard Dog', in a Mexican Standoff with Tommy, 'The Hun', yesterday afternoon. Neither of them would call it quits! It was ***One Tough Cookie*** against another."

There Are Other Fish In The Sea

there are other options besides this one....it is O.K. that you missed that opportunity, others will arise

Example: "Joe missed his chance to buy the car that he was so excited about. It did not bother him that much though. He knew that ***there were other fish in the sea***!"

Out Of Control

this idiom describes when something (or someone) is unmanageable, frenzied, wild, and unruly

Example: "Ella's dog needs some serious training! I saw her out walking him and he was wreaking havoc in the neighborhood. To say that he was ***out of control*** would be an understatement!"

Out Of Hand

an American idiom that describes whenever somebody gets carried away or out of control

Example: "Charlie is a little out of control fixing things with duct tape. Yesterday I saw him fixing a chicken's broken leg with a splint and duct tape! Things are a bit ***out of hand*** at Charlie's place!

Out Of The Frying Pan, Into The Fire

to get out of one big problem, only to find yourself in a worse situation

Example: "When Jenkins asked to be transferred to another department, he got stuck with his old enemy, Big John! In a manner of speaking, Jenkins jumped ***out of the frying pan and into the fire***!"

Out On A Limb

to take a big chance (usually to help somebody else) that could result in disaster....(also known as "sticking your neck out")

Example: "Jose went ***out on a limb*** to help his best friend Felix!"

Pedal To The Metal

this idiom refers to a car driver who pushes the gas pedal all the way to the car's floor, so the automobile will go as fast as it can……(also known as "flooring it")……It has come to be used anytime anyone goes all out on any activity

Example: "Billy put the *pedal to the metal* when he spotted his girlfriend pulling into the car hop!"

Pigging Out

this idiom is used to describe whenever someone is eating like a pig…not using silverware…not using manners

Example: "Ralph is eating like an animal in the jungle! Didn't anybody ever teach him any manners? He just sits there ***stuffing his face*** and ***pigging out***!"

Poker Faced

this term describes anyone who is good at keeping their true feelings hidden....someone who hides what they know or feel with a stiff facial expression

Example: "Gamblin' Tex is a great poker player. He knows how to bluff his hand! He always has a trick up his sleeve. Anyone who plays cards with him will tell you that he is hard to read, and that he never folds. He's a ***poker faced*** card player!"

The Pot Calling The Kettle Black

anyone who calls someone else out for their behaviors, when they should be criticizing themselves for doing the same, exact behaviors

Example: "Jimmy is calling Dan a lazy loafer for not getting the job done on time. Jim should take a look at himself, before he makes that judgement call; that's just ***the pot calling the kettle black***!"

Pull Yourself Together

this American Idiom is used to tell someone who is really upset (and out of order) to calm down, relax, and collect their composure

Example: "Dad was really upset when he found out that someone had stolen his credit card and spent three thousand dollars! Mom had to tell him to calm down, that the bank would reimburse him for that theft. After that, Dad was able to ***pull himself together***."

Pulling Your Hair Out

to be so frustrated with a reoccurring problem that one cannot seem to fix....(also known as "at the end of your rope")

Example: "Mr. Berting was so upset with his sewing machine, that he felt like ***pulling his hair out***!"

Pushing Up Daisies

a kinder way of talking about being dead

Example: "Old man Jefferson passed away last night. He had been sick for a long time. His family members were all very sad. His youngest grandson told me that his grandfather will be ***pushing up daisies*** from now on!"

Put On The Back Burner

to put something on the back burner is to give it a lower priority than something else that is more important at that time

Example: "Zeek remembered that the rice he was cooking needed to simmer for forty minutes. So he ***put it on the back burner*** while he worked on the chicken l'orange!"

Quick Fix

a temporary remedy or solution to a problem that will get the job done

Example: "Charlie used duct tape to mend the broken handle on the spade shovel. It was a good idea for a temporary ***quick fix***! He's been using that shovel for weeks, since that fix, and it still does the job!"

Road Rage

this American idiom is used to describe whenever one driver thinks he (or she) owns the road, which leads to tension with another driver(who is just as bad or worse)

Example: "I couldn't believe my eyes today! I saw a blue-haired lady flip the bird at a milk truck driver, who was stalled-out at the traffic lights. That's just a bad case of impolite and discourteous ***road rage*** on her part!"

Robbing The Cradle

an American idiom that is used to describe a situation whenever an older man courts (or marries) a younger woman

Example: "Everyone that see's Raymond with Sue thinks that he is too old for her. Such judgmental people say he is ***robbing the cradle***. But they say it behind Sue's and Raymond's back."

Rubbernecking

this idiom refers to a person who is stretching their neck to see something that they have no business to see (the opposite to minding their own business)

Example: "Your sister almost caused a major accident out on the highway today. She slowed down to see some accident that happened on the other side of the interstate. Her ***rubbernecking*** could have caused another multi-car collision!"

Run Like The Wind

the wind is very quick and powerful, so a strong and powerful runner can be described as such

Example: "When Josselyn was five years old, she ran very quickly around the park with her little friends. Her grandfather would yell to her, '***Run like the wind***, Josselyn!' And she did."

Scoot Down

to go somewhere in a hurry

Example: "Dorothea asked Constantine to ***scoot down*** to the Newbury Butcher to get some hamburger for the evening cook-out."

Second Banana

this idiom describes a person who is second in charge ..... subordinate to the Top Banana

Example: "Alex thinks he is the boss around this place, but everyone knows he is ***second banana***, and not the real boss."

Second Wind

a sudden burst of new energy that comes after you have been exhausted

Example: "Charlie spotted the lost duct tape, on the old rolled and pleated auto seat, in the garage. He had been searching for that tape for hours. When he saw it, he felt a new energy within. He felt that something had given him a ***second wind***."

See Red

this American idiom describes whenever a person shows extreme anger

Example: "My uncle Al ***saw red*** when I told him I backed into his new truck! He had just driven it home and had parked it in the driveway."

See Saw

up and down movement or back and forth action (as when two teams are competing and the leading score keeps changing)

Example: "The game last night was a real barnburner. I held my breath the whole game. It was a real ***see saw*** event!"

See You Later

this idiom is something said whenever there is a parting …it is a way to say "Goodbye" …..("catch you later", "so long", "take it easy" are similar expressions)

Example: "That was uncle Bill on the phone. He needs some help getting his car to start. I have to go**!** I'll ***see you later*****!**""

Shooting The Breeze

to talk about anything just to take up time.....to waste time on any talk that wasn't really very important....small talk to pass the time

Example: "While Marty, Jimmy and Bill were waiting for the bus to arrive, they were ***shooting the breeze*** about this and that; nothing that was really important."

Shrimp

this idiom refers to a person or animal that is very small

Example: "Pee Wee Jones is so little. All the boys his age like his leadership abilities. They admire his courage and daring. They all follow him around because he knows how to have a good time getting into mischief! The gang calls him ***Shrimp***!"

Sidelined

to be upset, sad, and/or depressed because you are no longer taking an active part in the action

Example: "Officer Manahan was ***sidelined*** because of an injury on her job. Her partner felt badly that she had slipped on a banana peel, while chasing down a criminal."

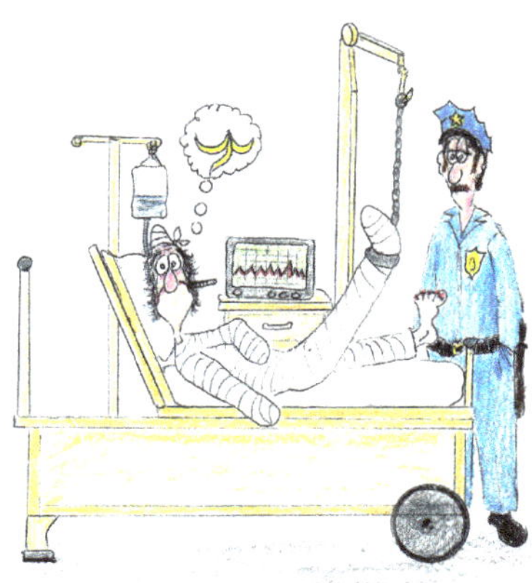

Silver Surfer

a phrase used to explain when an elderly person has learned to use the internet correctly

Example: “Old man Evens’ grandson has taught him how to use the internet to get information, and, to keep in touch with his friends. They all refer to him as the *Silver Surfer*!”

Sinking Ship

any company or organization that is doing poorly, in distress, or headed for bankruptcy or closure

Example: "Robert's employer had made some bad management decisions a short while ago. So Rob switched jobs because he felt that the company was ***a sinking ship***."

Something Smells Fishy

something is not right....something is wrong with this picture....somebody is up to no good

Example: "This car didn't have those two dents when I left it in the parking lot. ***Something smells fishy*** here."

Still Waters Run Deep

this idiom means that somebody can be more knowledgeable or emotional than he or she first appears to be....a silent person may be smarter that you think

Example: "Kip knows by his experience as a fisherman that ***still waters run deep***. Shallow water in a river runs fast, but deep water is usually calmer."

Stir Up A Hornet's Nest

to create a problem by uncovering something that lay hidden beneath the surface....to make someone furious and to get into deep trouble

Example: "James ***stirred up a hornet's nest*** when he brought up the Wall Street dilemma!"

Stretching The Truth

to exaggerate a story, to tell a story and stretch it way out of proportion, to say something that is not completely honest, to make something seem better that it really is

Example: "Josh was telling a story about the fish he caught last week. Everyone knew he has a history of ***stretching the truth***! No one believed him."

Take A Shot At Something

to try to do something that is challenging or difficult....and not to fear failure

Example: "The high school budget just couldn't be balanced. Mr. Brown stood up and volunteered to ***take a shot at it***, to see if he could make it happen!"

Take It Easy

a phrase that is used when saying "Goodbye"…. also known as "catch you later", "see you soon", "later", "see you"

Example: "When Jimbo and Bob left the card game, everyone yelled '***Take it easy***!'."

Take The Fall

to take the blame for something that he didn't do (also referred to as being the "fall guy")

Example: "Bill was eating his lunch in the cafeteria today, when the vice principal accused him of marking the tables with obscenities. Bill was not the guilty party, but he didn't argue. Instead, he ***took the fall*** for the real culprit, his friend Rob!."

Targeted

an American idiom that is used to describe whenever someone, or something, is focused upon for elimination or renewal (also known as "Zeroed In On")

Example: "The Mayor of Newburyport has ***targeted*** the waterfront for urban renewal!"

Teacher's Pet

this idiom is used to describe any student who is liked best by a teacher, and is given preferential treatment

Example: "Goodie Brown Nose is the favorite student in Mrs. Crabby"s English class. He always brings her a nice shiny red apple every school day. He is the ***teacher's pet***!"

The Blind Leading The Blind

.those who do not know how to do something, and who try to explain it to someone else

Example: "Ralph is showing Bob how to fix his dishwashing machine. Now that is what I call ***the blind leading the blind***! Ralph can't even change toilet paper. He doesn't have a mechanical bone in his body!"

The Cat's Ass

used to describe something spiffy…of superior quality…excellent…awesome…etc.

Example: "That new color t.v. that Dan bought for his family is ***the cat's ass***! I wish I had a television like that beauty."

The Facts Of Life

someone is taught the facts of life, they are learning about sex and reproduction

Example: "Father is out in the back room with Jacob. He is telling him about the ***facts of life***!"

The Only Free Cheese Is In The Mouse Trap

this idiom describes when someone thinks that they are getting something for free....they don't realize the real cost

Example: "Three mice went looking for food. They came upon two mouse traps. Immediately, the two quick mice jumped at the cheese, and were both killed. The third mouse had the good sense not to touch the cheese near those traps, until they had been sprung. He had all the cheese because he knew that ***the only free cheese is in the mouse trap***; that there is this no such thing as a free ride."

Through Thick And Thin

a phrase used to explain whenever a person is a good friend to another…always loyal and faithful and supportive

Example: "Ned and Tilly are really close. They have stuck together for all these years, through good times and bad times, ***through thick and thin***!"

Tip Of The Iceberg

this idiom means that only part of something can be seen, the rest of it is deep below the water's surface

Example: "Donald thinks this is going to be an easy job. He has no idea that what he is looking at is just ***the tip of the iceberg***. There is so much to do that Donald can't see!"

To Clam Up

to go silent…to shut up…to be quiet…to refuse to speak

Example: "Tom *clammed up*, when his wife asked him about what was shared, at the Gamblers Anonymous meeting!"

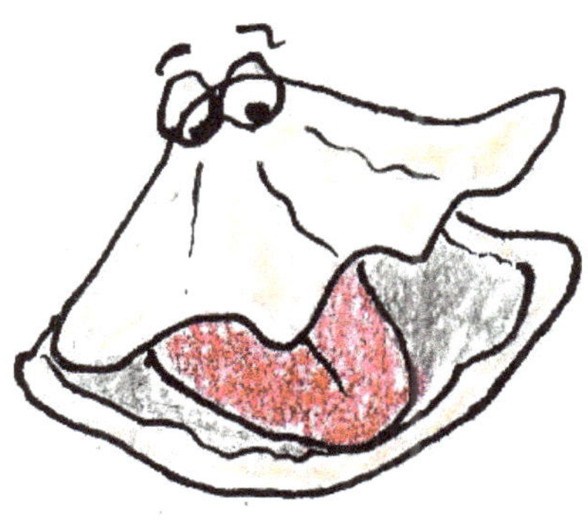

To Cut Class

also known as "to skip class" or "to ditch class" this American Idiom means to cut something out of your schedule without permission

Example: "Charlie went into the school's boiler room rather than to his Latin class in room 314. Don't you wonder what the attraction is down there that would cause someone to ***cut class***?"

To Get High

when a person uses intoxicants to achieve a state of mental euphoria (most often marijuana)

Example: "Our new neighbor spends a lot of time smoking something through a flexible hose from a funny looking vase-like container. I think he ***gets high*** from the experience!?

To Get Out Of Hand

to be in a situation that is out of your control....you can do nothing (or very little) about it

Example: "Kitty the cat got on top of the dog house and fell asleep at 11 o'clock in the morning. By the time she awoke, it was noon time and the sun had heated up the dog house roof. To make matters worse, Mad Dog Fido was awake, very hungry, and very mean spirited. How could things *get so out of hand*?"

To Miss The Boat

this idiom is used to describe whenever someone is too late for an activity

Example: "Jake was so busy talking to that good-looking girl, that he missed his bus for the game. I guess you could say ***he missed the boat.***"

To Wear Many Hats

this idiom comes from the days when craftsmen of different trades wore hats of their trade.....in America today, this is used to describe a person who does a variety of jobs

Example: "Bell is a valuable person at the office. She ***wears many hats***, and does everything to perfection!"

Two's Company, Three's A Crowd

a phrase used to explain whenever a third person wants to join two other people, there is an unwanted dynamic change…a third person will destroy the happiness and contentment of the couple

Example: "Mike and Jethro were down at the fishing hole, quietly enjoying the day. Loudmouth Ed showed up on the scene, and yelled that he was there to join them. Mike and Jethro felt like ***two's company, three's a crowd***!"

Under The Weather

an American Idiom that is used to describe whenever someone is not feeling well

Example: "Our top machinist doesn't look well today. I think he is a little bit ***under the weather***."

Up In Arms

this idiom is used to describe any person who is being or acting very grumpy or angry about something

Example: "Your uncle Carlton is ***up in arms*** about the new housing projects that the town is building next door to him!"

Wet Your Whistle

this idiom is used to describe whenever a person quenches their thirst with a drink

Example: "Bill usually can be found down at the Old Salt Café, after work, where he sits at the bar and ***wets his whistle*** !"

When The Cat's Away, The Mice Will Play

this idiom describes when no one in authority is present, everyone else can do whatever they want to do

Example: "Mister Maxx, the company's owner and manager, is on vacation down in Cuba. The rest of the factory workers are getting to work later, taking longer lunch breaks, and goofing-off for most of their work day. ***When the cat's away, the mice will play!***"

Get Up On The Wrong Side Of The Bed

this idiom describes whenever a person gets out of bed in a grouchy mood (and stays that way for the rest of the day)

Example: "Sam stepped in cat urine when he got up this morning. For the rest of the day he was grouchy; like a man who ***got up on the wrong side of the bed***."

You Are What You Eat

this idiom describes how people stay healthy or turn sickly through their diets

Example: "I saw Johnnie at the ice cream stand yesterday. He was eating a three-scooper! No wonder he is so overweight! *You are what you eat* from your head to your feet!!

You Can't Fight City Hall

this is an American Idiom that simply means that there is no way to beat a bureaucracy ……..(also known as "red tape")

Example: "Carl had a list of complaints that he took to the Mayor's Office at City Hall. The Mayor said there was nothing that could be done until it was presented to the City Council. The City Council couldn't meet until the following month. They would see what they could do at that time. ***You can't fight city hall***."

You Can't Judge A Book By Its Cover

one cannot judge the quality or character of someone else, or something else, by appearances only

Example: "Dave and Irvin are upset that they didn't pick Shorty for their basketball team. They just found out that he was last year's Slam Dunk King. They learned, the hard way, that ***you can't judge a book by its cover***!"

CPSIA information can be obtained
at www.ICGtesting.com
Printed in the USA
LVHW010904011221
704874LV00008B/266

9 781088 000366